Only Companion

ONLY COMPANION

Japanese Poems of Love
and Longing

Translated by Sam Hamill

SHAMBHALA
Boston & London
1992

Shambhala Publications, Inc.
Horticultural Hall
300 Massachusetts Avenue
Boston, Massachusetts 02115

Shambhala Publications, Inc.
Random Century House
20 Vauxhall Bridge Road
London SW1V 2SA

9 8 7 6 5 4 3 2 1
First Edition
Printed in Korea on acid-free paper
Distributed in the United States by Random House, Inc., in Canada by Random House of Canada Ltd, and in the United Kingdom by the Random Century Group
ISBN: 0-87773-647-2   LC: 91-50363

For William Anthony O'Daly
     Galen Garwood
     Greg Mitchell

     Tree Swenson and Eron Hamill

Contents

Preface

ANTHOLOGIES of a hundred poems have been commonplace in Japan for centuries. Indeed, one such anthology, *Hyakunin Isshū*, one poem each from one hundred poets, is studied and memorized by every young student in the country, and even provides the foundation for a popular card game. My own interest in Japanese poetry dates from publication of another great anthology, Kenneth Rexroth's *One Hundred Poems from the Japanese*, published by New Directions in 1957.

My translations of the poems in *Only Companion* were begun while on a Japan-U.S.

Fellowship in 1988. I spent several months taking advantage of the splendid library at International House in Tokyo, research that opened many corridors. Beginning with the first imperial anthology, *Man'yōshū*, compiled in the eighth century, I retraced the development of Japanese poetry and its critical vocabulary into the twentieth century, copying poems into my notebooks that seemed particularly available to translation. The poetry was in many ways familiar terrain, but at almost every step I discovered a new poem or poet I had overlooked during previous excursions.

Later, while roughly tracing Bashō's famous travel route through northern Honshu, I began translating the poems, often with the aid and inspiration of friends. There began to emerge two basic interlocking themes: the poem of romantic love and the poem of spiritual longing. Poems of changing seasons and passing years underscore a profound sense of temporality, while erotic poems and Zen poems, each in their own way, seek a state of transcendent grace.

These poems, made simply for the pleasure and epiphany of the process a poet identifies as *poesis*, become *something else* once they are gathered into a single volume. They represent a kind of collaborative gesture like that of Bashō's famous haiku:

Now I see her face,
the old woman, abandoned,
the moon her only companion.

Omokage ya
oba hitori naku
tsuki no tomo

The seer, the seen, the moon—these are not
three things, but one: a moment's epiphany,
a flash of *kenshō* or sudden illumination. But
the meaning, the authentic experience of the
poem, lies only within ourselves. And be-
gins with the quality of our listening.

It is a pleasure to acknowledge my debt
of gratitude to my Japanese translator, Keida
Yusuke, to our mutual friend Kawamura

Yoichi, and to my friends Aoki Shimpei and Ohmura Marie in Karuizawa. Thanks also to my old friends John and Sachi Solt. All have given me encouragement and inspiration even when my interpretations have run rather far afield. *Gasshō*.

Sam Hamill
Tokyo/Hanamaki-minami, 1988
Port Townsend, 1990

Only Companion

Wanting to preserve
the seeds of the human heart
for eternity
we return to the deep past—
the source of words in Japanese.

Tane to naru
hito no kokoro no
itsumo araba
mukashi ni oyobe
yamato koto no ha

—Kyōgoku Tamekane

My rocky journey
brings me a long way from home,
blown by autumn winds
that deliver freezing nights,
wild geese crying down the skies.

Ie sakari
tabi ni shi areba
akikaze no
samuki yube ni
gan nakiwataru

—Anonymous

Now the nights grow cold
and cold winds return to howl.
With you gone,
my whole life is torn by winds.
I wonder: Do you sleep alone?

Nagarauru
tsuma fuku kaze no
samuki yo ni
waga se no kimi wa
hitori ka nuramu

—Princess Yoza

Melancholy days,
traveling, filled with longing—
if I could not hear
the lonely cry of the crane,
it would be too much to bear.

Tabi ni shite
mono koishiki ni
tazu ga ne mo
kikoezariseba
koite shinamashi

—Takayasu no Ōshima

Traveling together,
that high mountain in autumn
was almost impassable.
How can you bravely hope
to make that journey alone?

Futari yukedo
yukisugigataki
akiyama wo
ika ni ka kimi ga
hitori koyuramu

—Princess Ōku

Men love to gossip,
and their every word is mean.
Now it comes to this:
at dawn I'll cross that river,
never again to be seen.

Hitogoto wo
shigemi kochitami
onoga yo ni
imada wataranu
asakawa wataru

—Princess Tajima

How does it happen?
I take this dried fish, your gift,
and go to the shore
and throw it into the ocean:
it rises and swims away.

Watatsumi no
oki ni mochiyukite
hanatsu tomo
uremu so kore ga
yomigaerinamu

—the priest Tsukan

If pressed to compare
this brief life, I might declare:
It's like the boat
that crossed this morning's harbor,
leaving no mark on the world.

Yo no naka wo
nani ni taoemu
asaborake
kogi yuku fune no
ato no shiranami

—the priest Mansei

Dusk, the Omi Sea,
a lone plover skimming waves,
and with each soft cry,
my heart too, like dwarf bamboo,
stirred, longing for bygone days.

Ōmi no umi
yūnami chidori
na ga nakeba
kokoro mo shinu ni
inishie omōyu

—Kakinomoto no Hitomaro

On the Eastern Moor
heat waves shimmer over ground.
I pause and look back:
suddenly, there it is again,
that same moon going down.

Himukashi no
no ni kagiroi no
tatsu miete
kaeri misureba
tsuki katabukinu

—Kakinomoto no Hitomaro

An ocean of clouds
rolls in waves across the sky,
carrying the moon
like a boat that disappears
into a thicket of stars.

Ame no umi ni
kumo no nami tachi
tsuki no fune
hoshi no hayashi ni
kogikakuru miyu

—Kakinomoto no Hitomaro

Endless autumn nights,
almost unbearably long,
are not long enough
for one to finally overcome
the loneliness of our love.

Aki no yo o
nagashi to iedomo
tsumorinishi
koi o tsukuseba
mijikaku arikeri

—Anonymous

When winter concludes,
it signals the birth of spring,
and the months and years
discover a renewed youth.
For a man, there's no such thing.

Fuyu sugite
haru shi kitareba
toshitsuki wa
arata naredomo
hito wa furiyuku

—Anonymous

Hold on a moment,
my little mountain cuckoo:
I have words for you:
say that I, too, grow weary,
exhausted by this world.

Yayoya mate
yamahototogisu
kotozutemu
ware yo no naka ni
sumiwabinu to yo

—Mikuni no Machi

Late evening finally comes:
I unlatch the door
and quietly await
the one
who greets me in my dreams.

Yu saraba
yado ake makete
ware matamu
ime ni aimi ni
komu tou hito o

—Otomo no Yakamochi

When my wife left home,
nothing at all could hold her.
Now she lies hidden
in the heart of the mountain
where my heart wanders alone.

Ie sakari
imasu wagimo o
todomekane
yamagakushitsure
kokorodo mo nashi

—Otomo no Yakamochi

From outside my house,
only the faint distant sound
of gentle breezes
wandering through bamboo leaves
in the long evening silence.

Wa ga yado no
isasamuratake
fuku kaze no
oto no kasokeki
kono yube ka mo

—Otomo no Yakamochi

Is it true my love
has finally come to see me,
or am I dreaming?
Am I sane? Or is she
an invention of my needing?

Utsutsu ni ka
imo ga kimaseru
yume ni ka mo
ware ka matoeru
koi no shigeki ni

—Anonymous

In summer mountains,
the one he loves so dearly
wanders on alone:
and then the shrill, piercing cry,
a cuckoo's melody.

Natsuyama ni
koishiki hito ya
irinikemu
koe furitatete
naku hototogisu

—Ki no Akimine

Don't let that cold wind
wailing down from the mountains
blow these leaves away:
I look on them with longing:
wind, don't sweep them away.

Koishiku wa
mite mo shinobamu
momijiba o
fuki na chirashi so
yamaoroshi no kaze

—Anonymous

Autumn has returned:
multicolored fallen leaves
carpet the garden,
and the long path lies buried:
no visitor wades those drifts.

Aki wa kinu
momiji wa yado ni
furishikinu
michi fumiwakete
tou hito wa nashi

—Anonymous

Under the sky's
broad reaches, like ice
imperceptibly melting,
may your cold heart
melt for me.

Haru tateba
kiyuru kori no
nokori naku
kimi ga kokoro wa
ware ni tokenamu

—Anonymous

Early morning glows
in the faint shimmer
of first light.
Choked with sadness,
I help you into your clothes.

Shinonome no
hogara hogara to
akeyukeba
ono ga kinuginu
naru zo kanashiki

—Anonymous

Angry river winds
grow bitter cold, so cold
this long winter's night,
going to see my lover,
even distant plovers cry.

Omoi kane
imo gari yukeba
fuyu no yo no
kawakaze samumi
chidori naku nari

—Ki no Tsurayuki

The flowering plum
blossoms, filled with spring brilliance,
which we recognize
from our mountain of darkness,
traveling alone, without light.

Ume no hana
niou harube wa
kurabuyama
yami ni koyuredo
shiruku zo arikeru

—Ki no Tsurayuki

The cherry blossoms
linger in the wind's wide wake
where they were scattered,
dancing in circles and waves
across a waterless sky.

Sakurabana
chirinuru kaze no
nagori ni wa
mizu naki sora ni
nami zo tachikeru

—Ki no Tsurayuki

Now that he's let go
of those flowers he tried to hold
with his springtime song,
the little warbler's silent.
Uninspired, he'll sing no more.

Nakitomuru
hana shi nakereba
uguisu mo
hate wa monouku
narinubera nari

—Ki no Tsurayuki

Approaching midnight
on a hillside, in springtime,
in a temple hall,
even in my deepest dreams,
the blossoms continue to fall.

Yadori shite
haru no yamabe ni
netaru yo wa
yume no uchi ni mo
hana zo chirikeru

—Ki no Tsurayuki

So high in the mountains,
you must be lonely,
blossoming cherry:
no one to sing your glory.
I will praise you if I can.

Yama takami
hito mo susamenu
sakurabana
itaku na wabi so
ware mihayasamu

—Anonymous

How mysterious!
The lotus remains unstained
by its muddy roots,
delivering shimmering
bright jewels from common dew.

Hachisuba no
nigori ni shimanu
kokoro mote
nani ka wa tsuyu o
tama to azamuku

—the monk Henjō

Poetic justice?
I stand alone with my thoughts
as the crickets cry,
wild pink mountain blossoms
swirling in gathering dusk.

Ware nomi ya
aware to omowamu
kirigirisu
naku yukage no
yamatonadeshiko

—the monk Sosei

Where is the dark seed
that grows the forget-you plant?
Searching, now I see
it grows in the frozen heart
of one who has murdered love.

Wasuregusa
nani o ka tane to
omoishi wa
tsurenaki hito no
kokoro narikeri

—the monk Sosei

Dawn has almost come,
and yet the evening lingers,
this rainy season.
In what corridors of cloud
does the moon find its hotel?

Natsu no yo wa
mada yoi nagara
akenuru o
kumo no izuko ni
tsuki nokoru ran

—Kiyohara Fukayabu

The world beyond clouds
is not foreign to my soul—
it won't leave you now.
We speak of separation—
but that's only illusion.

Kumoi ni mo
kayou kokoro no
okureneba
wakaru to hito ni
miyu bakari nari

—Kiyohara Fukayabu

Yours is not a song
we hear only once in a while,
little cuckoo.
Though we listen all our lives,
your every song surprises.

Mazurashiki
koe naranaku ni
hototogisu
kokora no toshi o
akazu mo aru ka na

—Ki no Tomonori

Crossing Otowa
Mountain in early morning,
a single cuckoo
in a distant tree, lonely—
its song a high, piercing cry.

Otowayama
kesa koekureba
hototogisu
kozue haruka ni
ima zo naku naru

—Ki no Tomonori

In the high bare limbs
of twisted trees, the moon
slowly awakens
to the soul's darkest season:
inevitable autumn.

Ko no ma yori
morikuru tsuki no
kage mireba
kokorozukushi no
aki wa kinikeri

—Anonymous

Autumn's consequence
is not mine alone: nothing
can be done with it.
Still I am deeply saddened
by the shrill song of crickets.

Wa ga tame ni
kuru aki ni shi mo
aranaku ni
mushi no ne kikeba
mazu zo kanashiki

—Anonymous

No one ever traced
the root of melancholy
to turning seasons.
These lonely autumn nights, we
sink, nonetheless, in misery.

Itsu wa to wa
toki wa wakanedo
aki no yo zo
mono omou koto no
kagiri narikeri

—Anonymous

Looking at the moon,
a thousand heavy sorrows
weigh down upon me.
It can't be—for me alone
these barren autumns return.

Tsuki mireba
chiji ni mono koso
kanashikere
wa ga mi hitotsu no
aki ni wa aranedo

—Ōe no Chisato

Lonely cricket-cries
from the paulownia tree—
these long autumn nights
bring back a thousand sorrows,
every note a knife through me.

Kirigirisu
itaku na naki so
aki no yo no
nagaki omoi wa
ware zo masareru

—Fujiwara no Tadafusa

In bare autumn fields,
the pine-crickets call, "We wait,
we wait." If I go
out to answer them, I'll cry,
"Am I the one? Is it me?"

Aki no no ni
hito matsumushi no
koe su nari
ware ka to yukite
iza toburawamu

—Anonymous

Hearing cicadas
cry long in hills at twilight,
I mistake shadows
of these mountains for nightfall,
I hear evening in their song.

Higurashi no
nakitsuru nabe ni
hi wa kurenu
to omou wa yama no
kage ni zo arikeru

—Anonymous

Cicadas sing
high in their mountain homes
and evening gathers
its darkness. Only the wind—
no one else will ever come.

Higurashi no
naku yamazato no
yugure wa
kaze yori hoka ni
tou hito mo nashi

—Anonymous

In my mountain home,
autumn's steady procession:
the loneliest hour.
I lie awake in the dark,
a stag's cry piercing my heart.

Yamazato wa
aki koso koto ni
wabishikere
shika no naku ne ni
me o samashitsutsu

—Mibu no Tadamine

Born on autumn nights,
the dewdrops remain dewdrops,
but the wide meadows
on the mountainside all shine,
washed by tears of passing geese.

Aki no yo no
tsuyu o ba tsuyu to
oki nagara
kari no namida ya
nobe o somuramu

—Mibu no Tadamine

Lonely autumn moon
in multicolored foliage:
with the stag's sharp cry
you return all our sorrows,
you return our hour of gloom.

Okuyama ni
momiji fumiwake
naku shika no
koe kiku toki zo
aki wa kanashiki

—Anonymous

Now autumn bush clover
turns all the autumn colors,
those who live alone
must find it difficult
to sleep through the night till dawn.

Akihagi no
shitaba irozuku
ima yori ya
hitori aru hito no
inegate ni suru

—Anonymous

Traveling this road,
one suspicious eye
watches the maidenflowers:
here, on a mountain named Man,
they prosper and multiply.

Ominaeshi
ushi to mitsutsu zo
yukisuguru
otokoyama ni shi
tateri to omoeba

—Furu no Imamichi

The maidenflower
bends to every autumn wind
and I must wonder:
to whom does she give her heart
here in the late fall meadow?

Ominaeshi
aki no nokaze ni
uchinabiki
kokoro hitotsu o
tare ni yosuramu

—Fujiwara no Tokihira

Filled with his longing,
the stag cries from the mountain:
he is unaware
of the fields where he roams:
blossoming maidenflowers.

Tsuma kouru
shika zo naku naru
ominaeshi
ono ga sumu no no
hana to shirazu ya

—Ōshikōchi no Mitsune

Each grass and each tree
takes on a hundred colors.
For these white flowers
blooming on the tossing sea,
there is no autumn season.

Kusa mo ki mo
iro kawaredomo
watatsuumi no
nami no hana ni zo
aki nakarikeru

—Fun'ya no Yasuhide

I cannot ask you
when, exactly, you plan to leave.
Surely, when you go,
like a single drop of dew,
I will vanish from this world.

Karakoromo
tatsu hi wa kikaji
asatsuyu no
okite shi yukeba
kenubeki mono o

—Anonymous

In the long evening,
under the edge of purple clouds,
I long to meet one
who has gone to wander
the latitudes of heaven.

Yugure wa
kumo no hatate ni
mono zo omou
amatsusora naru
hito o kou tote

—Anonymous

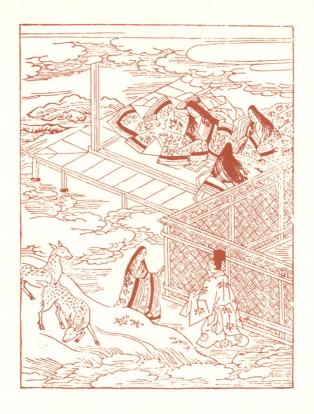

As night follows night,
I shift and turn my pillow,
my eyes open wide.
Long ago I dreamed of you.
How was I sleeping that night?

Yoi yoi ni
makura sadamemu
kata mo nashi
ika ni neshi yo ka
yume ni miekemu

—Anonymous

In river shallows,
duckweed continues to grow,
unseen by water.
Likewise, my love too shall flow,
though it remains unseen by you.

Kawa no se ni
nabiku tamamo no
migakurete
hito ni shirarenu
koi mo suru ka na

—Ki no Tomonori

The soft autumn winds
bring echoes of a koto
played in the distance.
Why must that whispered refrain
remind me I love in vain?

Akikaze ni
kakinasu koto no
koe ni sae
hakanaku hito no
koishikaruramu

—Mibu no Tadamine

Like river grasses
wandering currents, rootlessly
drifting, I'm driven
by someone else's whims,
propelled by her storms, her winds.

Tagitsu se ni
nezashi todomenu
ukikusa no
ukitaru koi mo
ware wa suru ka na

—Mibu no Tadamine

These cold mountain winds
blow white clouds to their ends
far from these dark peaks.
But where, my love, is the end
of the cold winds of your heart?

Kaze fukeba
mine ni wakaruru
shirakumo no
taete tsurenaki
kimi ga kokoro ka

—Mibu no Tadamine

As pale daylight breaks,
I start for the long road home.
Walking in heartache,
first teardrops and then raindrops
soak through the sleeves of my robe.

Akenu tote
kaeru michi ni wa
kokitarete
ame mo namida mo
furisobochitsutsu

—Fujiwara no Toshiyuki

Our meetings are brief—
kisses stolen in closets.
People love to gossip
like the Yoshino Rapids
love the crash and roar of water.

Au koto wa
tama no o bakari
na no tatsu wa
yoshino no kawa no
tagitsu se no goto

—Anonymous

I worried: might you
come here; might I go there;
might we meet again?
Then, at last, the bashful moon:
I slept with my door unlatched.

Kimi ya komu
ware ya yukamu no
isayoi ni
maki no itado mo
sasazu nenikeri

—Anonymous

So many reasons
why I must question your love,
your sincerity:
now my sorrows fall like rain,
fall harder, gaining fury.

Kazukazu ni
omoi omowazu
toigatami
mi o shiru ame wa
furi zo masareru

—Ariwara no Narihira

Is that the same moon?
Is this the same old springtime,
the same ancient spring?
And is this not my body,
the same body you once knew?

Tsuki ya aranu
haru ya mukashi no
haru naranu
wa ga mi hototsu wa
moto no mi no shite

—Ariwara no Narihira

Returning again
and again like endless waves,
my heart is stolen
by memories of a stranger
who carries it away.

Tachikaeri
aware to zo omou
yoso nite mo
hito ni kokoro o
okitsu shiranami

—Ariwara no Motokata

These harsh autumn winds
can't penetrate a body,
hard as they might blow.
How is it your heart was blown
down the far reach of heaven?

Akikaze wa
mi o wakete shi mo
fukanaku ni
hito no kokoro no
sora ni naruramu

—Ki no Tomonori

I still continue,
an eternal outsider,
my life transparent
as this cold, clear morning air,
not one cloud in this wide sky.

Kumo mo naku
nagitaru asa no
ware nare ya
itowarete nomi
yo o ba henuramu

—Ki no Tomonori

Now I go to live
among trails deep in mountains.
The day will not come
when my black sleeves are not soaked
through with tears of my mourning.

Ashibiki no
yamabe ni ima wa
sumizome no
koromo no sode no
hiru toki mo nashi

—Anonymous

True, I may appear
unkempt like a rotting tree,
jetsam or flotsam,
but on the right occasion
this old heart can still blossom.

Katachi koso
miyamagakure no
kuchiki nare
kokoro wa hana ni
nasaba narinamu

—the monk Kengei

Did I once believe
I could come to this?—reeling
in a fishing line,
in exile, in a province,
and not one friend to be seen.

Omoiki ya
hina no wakare ni
otoroete
ama no nawa taki
isari semu to wa

—Takamura no Ason

Where shall I turn now
when I am in need of a friend?
At Takasago,
even aging stately pines
cannot replace lost friends.

Tare o ka mo
shiru hito ni semu
takasago no
matsu mo mukashi no
tomo naranaku ni

—Fujiwara Okikaze

I long for him most
during these long moonless nights.
I lie awake, hot,
the growing fires of passion
bursting, blazing in my heart.

Hito ni awamu
tsuki no naki ni wa
omoi okite
mune hashiribi ni
kokoro yake ori

—Ono no Komachi

It's not a dewdrop—
it is only this old heart
settling on a flower.
But now it quakes and trembles
at each new breeze, every hour.

Tsuyu naranu
kokoro o hana ni
okisomete
kaze fuku goto ni
monoomoi zo tsuku

—Ki no Tsurayuki

My black hair tangled
as my own tangled thoughts,
I lie here alone,
dreaming of one who has gone,
who stroked my hair till it shone.

Kurogami no
midarete shirazu
uchifuseba
mazu kakiyarishi
hito zo koishiki

—Izumi Shikibu

Transparent spring rains
from here to the horizon
fall on grass and trees,
beginning to dye everything
in shades of deep spring green.

Harusame wa
konomo kanomo no
kusa mo ki mo
wakezu midori ni
somuru nariken

—Fujiwara Shunzei

By morning, the leaves
have fallen into silence,
the wind has finally parted,
like lovers after a night,
all talked out, now broken-hearted.

Asa goto ni
koe o osamuru
kaze no oto wa
yo o hete karuru
hito no kokoro ka

—Saigyō

No one visits here
in my dark mountain hut
where I live alone.
But for this sweet loneliness,
it would be too bleak to bear.

Tou hito mo
omoitaetaru
yamazato no
sabishisa nakuba
sumiukaramashi

—Saigyō

Deep within the mountains,
the mind's moon brightly shines,
its light mirroring
all things everywhere, itself
mirrored in the enlightened mind.

Fukaki yama ni
kokoro no tsuki shi
suminureba
kogami ni yomo no
satori o zo miru

—Saigyō

Dead, I'll lie forever
alone beneath a blanket
of cold moss
remembering what is learned
only from dew and dark stone.

Shi nite fusamu
koke no mushiro o
omou yori
kanete shiraruru
iwakage no tsuyu

—Saigyō

Needing a pillow,
where shall I find grasses
that I can bind?
Wherever I'm bound to go,
this evening moor is home.

Makura tote
izure no kusa ni
chigiru ran
yuku o kagiri no
nobe no yugure

—Kamo no Chōmei

Under heavy snow,
bamboo groans and cracks all night—
I waken in Fushimi
from dreams of paths to love
that also now lie buried.

Yume kayou
michi sae taenu
kuretake no
Fushimi no sato no
yuki no shitaore

—Fujiwara Ariie

Call it loneliness,
that deep, beautiful color
no one can describe:
over these dark mountains,
the gathering autumn dusk.

Sabishisa wa
sono iro to shi mo
nakarikeri
maki tatsu yama no
aki no yugure

—the priest Jakuren

From over the moors,
the wind stirs the pampas grass
along this narrow road,
and the evening sun grows cold,
and autumn begins to close.

Nobe toki
obana ni kaze wa
fukimichite
samuki yuhi ni
aki zo kureyuku

—Jusammi Chikako

Like a bird's sky-road
which leaves no trail in the air,
my life, too, shall go
unnoticed, and if I cry,
will anyone know or care?

Tori no michi no
ato naki mono o
omoitachite
hitori shi nakedo
hito shirameya mo

—Kyōgoku Tamekane

Once my bitterness
has found its way into words,
it dissipates,
running deep into my heart,
anger replaced by sadness.

Koto no ha ni
idete urami wa
tsukihatete
kokoro ni komuru
usa ni narunuru

—Kyōgoku Tamekane

Sometimes I wonder
what thoughts, what feelings he knew
as he was leaving.
Tell me what you remember,
poor cold, silent autumn moon.

Ika narishi
hito no nasake ka
omoiizuru
koshitkata katare
aki no yo no tsuki

—Kyōgoku Tamekane

Late spring memories
flood over me as I watch,
day's wind now dying,
the evening beach where you rowed
away, leaving me crying.

Haru no nagori
nagamuru ura no
yunagi ni
kogiwakareyuku
fune mo urameshi

—Kyōgoku Tamekane

So you must persist
in asking where my heart goes
all the long, cold night.
Like following trails left by birds
who vanished with yesterday's sky.

Yo mo sugara
kokoro no yukue
tazunereba
kino no sora ni
tobu tori no ato

—Kōhō Kennichi

Here in a thatched hut
hidden among mountain peaks,
with barely room for one,
I'm suddenly invaded
by wandering white clouds.

Ware dani mo
sebashi to omou
kusa no io ni
nakaba shashiiru
mine no shiragumo

—Kōhō Kennichi

"Satori" noted,
the mind, like quicksilver, goes,
falsely "enlightened,"
down those old wrong-headed roads,
each more wrong than one before.

Satori tote
tsune ni wa kawaru
kokoro koso
mayoi no naka no
mayoi narikere

—Musō Soseki

If only people
would not come to visit me
in lonely mountains
where I have built my retreat
from the world's many trials.

Tou hito mo
omoitaetaru
yamazato no
sabishisa nakuba
sumuikaramashi

—Musō Soseki

Sometimes, while wandering,
when I cannot find which road
leads back the way I came,
the road goes anywhere,
and anywhere at all is home.

Furusato to
sadamuru kata no
naki toki wa
izuku ni yuku mo
ieji nerikeri

—Musō Soseki

At Point Ozaki
the early morning breeze
is slowly tamed:
from Tashima Island,
the voice of a thousand cranes.

Ozaki no
ura fuku kaze no
asanagi ni
Tashima o wataru
tsuru no morogoe

—Imagawa Ryōshun

Without beginning,
utterly without end,
the mind is born
to struggles and distresses,
and dies—and that is emptiness.

Hajime naku
owari mo naki ni
waga kokoro
umare shisuru
mo ku no ku nari

—Ikkyū Sōjun

The moon is a house
in which the mind is master.
Look very closely:
only impermanence lasts.
This floating world, too, will pass.

Tsuki wa ie
kokoro wa nushi to
miru toki wa
nao kari no yo no
sumai naru keri

—Ikkyū Sōjun

And what is mind
and how is it recognized?
It is clearly drawn
in sumi ink, the sound
of breezes drifting through pine.

Kokoro towa
ikanaru mono wo
iu yaran
sumie ni kakishi
matsukaze no oto

—Ikkyū Sōjun

Everyone's journey
through this world is the same,
so I won't complain.
Here on the plains of Nasu
I place my trust in the dew.

Nagakeji yo
kono yo wa tare mo
uki tabi to
omoinasu no no
tsuyu ni makasete

—Sōgi

Now what can I do?
My writing hand in a cast
is useless—
can't manipulate chopsticks,
can't even wipe my ass!

Ika ni sen
mono kakisusabu
te wa okite
hashi toru koto to
shiri noguu koto

—Sōchō

How utterly vain!
The great old men of China
arguing reason
before they can articulate
the origin of things.

Kusuwashiki
kotowari shirazute
Karahito no
mono no kotowari
toku ga hakanasa

—Motoori Norinaga

Coming to visit
the Western Capital's
old, crumbling ruins,
listen: Han Shan's temple bell,
in the evening, tolling.

Arehateshi
nishi no miyako ni
kite mireba
Kanzeonji no
irai no kane

—Sengai Gibbon

Was it all a dream—
I mean those old bygone days—
were they what they seemed?
All night long I lie awake
listening to autumn rain.

Somo kami wo
omoeba yume ka
utsutsu ka mo
yoru wa shigure no
ame wo kikitsutsu

—Ryōkan

What might I leave you
as a last gift when my time comes?
Springtime flowers,
the cuckoo singing all summer,
the yellow leaves of autumn.

Katami tote
nani ka nokosan
haru wa hana
natsu hototogisu
aki wa momijiba

—Ryōkan

Following his bath,
I gave my handsome lover
my best purple robe
to keep him from the cold.
He blushed, and was beautiful.

Yuagari o
mikaze mesuna no
waga uwagi
enjimurasaki
hito utsukushiki

—Yosano Akiko

The handsome boatman
singing, floating the river,
fills me with longing—
he's thrilled just remembering
last night's port-of-call girl.

Haru no kawa
noriai-bune no
wakaki ko ga
yobe no tomari no
uta netamashiki

—Yosano Akiko

All alone
beside the temple bell:
I stole away
to secretly meet you here.
But now the fog has cleared.

So to nukete
sono moya ochite
hito o mizu
yube no kane no
katae sabishiki

—Yosano Akiko

By a nameless stream—
small and very beautiful,
last night spent alone—
these broad desolate fields
in a harsh summer dawn.

Koi naranu
nezame tatazumu
no no hirosa
nanashi ogawa no
utsukushiki natsu

—Yosano Akiko

All "three thousand worlds"
are summoned here together
by this falling snow,
this snow that lightly covers
all three thousand worlds and more.

Awayuki no
naka ni tachitaru
michiochi
mata sono naka ni
awayuki zo furu

—Ryōkan

The mind is all sky,
the heart utterly empty,
and the perfect moon
is completely transparent
entering western mountains.

Yami harete
kokoro no sora ni
sumu tsuki wa
nishi no yamabe ya
chikaku naruran

—Saigyō

Afterword

EARLY JAPANESE POETRY is a highly refined poetry of sensibility. Technically, the verse form should be identified as *tanka,* but at the time of the tenth-century anthology *Kokinshū,* the more generic *waka* was still customarily used. The language is most often simple, often misleadingly so. It is formal in diction; it uses certain devices like the "pillow word," or *makura kotoba* (a fixed epithet), and "cutting word," or "pivot word"—*kakekotoba,* a word play based on homophones creating a plurisignation; it is thematically restricted; and it is dependent more upon emotional *quality* than upon mere personality. The language of waka—which means simply "Japanese poem"—is far less dense than that of Chinese poetry, its taproot probably located somewhere deep in preliterate folk song. But tanka grew quite apart from the folk poetry tradition; continuing and refining the high courtly tradition established by the *Man'yōshū* poets, it became, increasingly, a poetry of great subtlety and sophistication.

Kakinomoto no Hitomaro, eighth-century court poet and the greatest poet of the *Man'yōshū*, is one of those responsible for perfecting and refining the form, often in envoy (*hanka*) footnoting his longer poems or *chōka*. Waka, by the time of *Kokinshū*, was court poetry, written by nearly all formally educated literati; it came to be used as a tool for discreet communication, for the endless games of seduction within the courts, for elegies and laments, in poetry-writing contests, or for simple celebrations of turning seasons, and later, for the expression of Buddhist insight.

Although early Japanese poets were steeped in Chinese poetics, tanka retained an essentially Japanese character—quite different from the shorter classical Chinese verse forms with four lines of five or seven characters each. This, despite efforts by classical poets such as Ōe no Chisato to create "tanka" by translating Chinese poems into Japanese form. Chisato's translations rarely rose above the level of mundane prose. The tradition he hoped to begin ended for all practical purposes with his own compositions. Nevertheless, Japanese poets were fond of comparing tanka to four-line, five-character Chinese poems, compiling anthologies (like the *Roeishū*, compiled several decades after the *Kokinshū*) arranged by season and subject.

The Japanese poet generally preferred the accessibility and lyricism of Li T'ai-po to the dense, powerful humanity and formal genius of Tu Fu—and the more courtly poetry of Po Chu-i to either of those two. But with few exceptions, classical Japanese poets expressed their Chinese influences by writing poems in *kanji,* or Chinese language, and in traditional Chinese forms.

The seventh and eighth centuries were a period of enormous Chinese cultural influence within Japan, beginning with an official mission to China in 607 and concluding with the shift of the (first) capital from Nara to Nagaoka. Students and priests traveled to and from China, Buddhism began to flourish in Japan, and Chinese arts and crafts from painting and music to embroidery and architecture became the model for Japanese artisans in the city. Even the city of Nara itself was modeled on the T'ang capital at Ch'ang-an. In 770, the empress Shotoku ordered one million pagodas built in Buddhist temples across the country, each to contain a small printed charm. Many scholars believe this to be the introduction of printing to Japan. All official documents were composed in a Sino-Japanese hybrid language, as was all scholarly work. And any object or composition that carried the word *kara* ("Chinese") was thought to be marked with the indelible handprint of elegance.

This worshipful attitude toward Chinese philosophy and aesthetics, begun with the arrival of the *Analects* of Confucius in the sixth century, was intensified through the profound influence of the great Buddhist teacher Kōbō Daishi (also called Kūkai, 774–835), who founded the Shingon or True Word sect in Japan and who had apprenticed himself in China under the Buddhist teacher Hui Kuo. Kōbō Daishi became head of what was essentially a Buddhist aristocracy. During this period, both the Japanese court and Buddhist society soaked up Chinese influence like sponges. The *Man'yōshū* has but a single reference to plum blossom scent among its 4500 poems, but the 116 *kanshi* (poems written in Chinese) collected in the *Kaifūsō* in 751 include five such poems. By the early tenth century, plum blossoms were standard imagery for seasonal poems. Snow on plum blossoms became a "pillow word." The plum blossom with all its aesthetic associations would become as "Japanese" as the set imagery associated with the moon and stars over Sado Island several hundred years later.

By the time Ki no Tsurayuki wrote his *kana* (Japanese-language) preface to the 1111 tanka of the *Kokinshū* in 905, Japan was once again internalizing the vast influences it had actively sought during the previous two hundred years. The Japanese tended to alternate fascination with foreign cultures with intense internalization and introspection, as Ivan Morris noted in his excellent study of Heian (Kokinshū) culture, *The World of the Shining Prince* (New York: Penguin, 1979).

By the time of Lady Murasaki, poetry—practically all literature—was written in *kanabungaku,* a phonetic alphabet that was at times identified by heavy-handed Sinologues as "women's writing," thanks largely to the power and grace of Murasaki herself and to the elegant tanka of Ono no Komachi. There are essentially no Chinese characters in *Genji monagatari.* While tanka (and prose) composed by women tended to be written exclusively in *kana* (women were forbidden access to Chinese studies), those composed by men often combined phonetic *kana* with Chinese characters. The idea that *kana* is exclusively "women's language" is largely misleading; it was used widely by writers of both genders.

Before Bashō invigorated the form three hundred years ago, *haiku* existed only as *hokku,* the opening verse of the *renga,* a poem written by multiple authors at popular poetry-writing contests. The three-line, seventeen-syllable haiku is probably more directly indebted to Chinese verse than to tanka. It may be the result of having lengthened the second line a couple of syllables, then dropping the third line completely, using the "cutting word" to set up a conception of infinite evocation. The primary Japanese poetic critical vocabulary grew out of the tanka tradition. Even to this day, many Japanese poets observe, "Haiku began and ended with Bashō." Brought into historical perspective, haiku is at best a minor verse form associated properly with the literature of Zen. Tanka, on the other hand, has been *the* sustaining verse form in Japanese poetry for well over a thousand years.

During the nearly nine hundred years since the *Kokinshū* was compiled, tanka has been in and out of fashion. It has accommodated the profound silences of Zen and the polite hypocrisy of otherwise brilliant court poets, the heart-rending loneliness of devastated families and the exquisite tears of young love, and the didactic, tutelary observations of political and religious poets, returning us time and again to the natural world and to our own sense of diurnal, even momentary temporality within it.

From the 1920s until the end of World War II, hundreds, indeed thousands of Japanese poets cranked out tanka in support of Japanese nationalism, creating a backlash against the very form itself by more worldly literati. There were "anti-tanka" literary journals, and certain "modernist" poets refused to have anything to do with any poet who wrote in the form. In some cases, it was the equivalent of blaming Wagner for Nazism. However, it might be compared to the sonnet in English verse: just as the form appears to be utterly exhausted, something or someone reinvigorates it. Like the sonnet in English, the tanka in Japanese has become a form of understanding within a musical structure.

Arthur Waley, using the generic term *uta*, or song, to describe the thirty-one-syllable tanka or waka form, says in *Japanese Poetry* (London: The Clarendon Press, 1919), "It is not possible that the rest of the world will ever realize the importance of Japanese poetry, because of all poetries it is the most completely untranslatable. Its beauty consists in the perfection with which a thought and a *body of sound* [my emphasis] are fitted into a small rigid frame. An *uta* runs into its mould like quicksilver into a groove. In translation, only the thought survives; the poem no longer 'goes', any more than a watch goes if you take its works out of their casing and empty them upon a sheet of paper."

The Japanese syllabary (beginning with the memorization of *ah, o-o-o, i-i-i, eh, oh; kah, koo, ki, keh, ko;* and so on) echoes perfectly ordinary syllables within our own language. For a Westerner, making these sounds is far, far more simple than tackling the subtle complexities of the rising, falling, and level tones of Chinese. And as Arthur Waley, Kenneth Rexroth, Burton Watson, and others have more than adequately demonstrated, the English "equivalent" of the original can indeed "go" once the translator finds the heart of the *experience* of the poem.

In new American dress, these poems lose much of their historical context. The naive Western reader will not recognize certain allusions, nor certain resonances, and will surely be unfamiliar with some cultural and linguistic phenomena. Made with the intention of being heard, the poems come without footnotes and without commentary. Great scholarship in English is readily available in Helen Craig McCollough's monumental study of the *Kokinshū*, in her several other scholarly studies and translations, and elsewhere. Plentifully available:

Earl Miner's *Introduction to Japanese Court Poetry* (Stanford, Calif.: Stanford University Press, 1968), provides an excellent short foundation in pre-sixteenth-century Japanese poetics; and Kenneth Rexroth's *One Hundred Poems from the Japanese* (New York: New Directions, 1957) includes an excellent essay on Japanese poetry. *From the Country of Eight Islands,* edited by Burton Watson and Hiroaki Sato (Seattle: University of Washington Press, 1981), is *the* master anthology of our time. I have published an appreciation of Japanese poetics and my own sense of *kadō,* the way of poetry, *Bashō's Ghost* (Seattle: Broken Moon Press, 1989), that includes a substantial bibliography of works in English.

It has been my practice to attempt to make an equivalent poem in American English, emphasizing the totality of the whole poem over *verbo verbum* analysis. Certain vowels within the original poem sometimes suggest key rhymes or repeated vowel sounds. At other times, *logopoeia* seems more important than *melopoeia*, and I simply lay a melodic base through which the images are clarified. I make no use of any inflexible theory or practice except to consistently respect the integrity of the line, *each* line, in composition. Nor did the original poets restrict themselves to an absolute syllabic measure: some tanka may vary by as much as four or five syllables. And it has been my practice to respect the order of imagery in

the original as much as lyrical syntax per-
mits. In some instances I have felt it neces-
sary to add a word or two to the poem,
sometimes in the form of a gloss, at other
times a modifier to fill out the sound and
rhythm. Part of the translator's art is inter-
pretative.

Writing more than eight hundred years
ago, Saigyō said:

> He whose heart and soul
> are at one with the great Void
> steps into the mist
> and suddenly thinks himself
> stepping right out of this world.

Sora ni naru
kokoro wa haru no
kasumi nite
yo ni araji tomo
omoitatsu kana

And yet we are *in* this world. Eight centuries later, the "truth of the poem" remains as vital, as necessary, as illuminating as the day it was written. Saigyō would no doubt be pleased, even delighted, to learn that his poem in translation calls to mind a very famous poem by the late James Wright. Japanese poetry is embroidered with such echoes and paraphrases, called *honkadori*. Finally, his poem returns us to the *real* world, a world articulated in a few noble and simple and essential ideas.

The cry of the stag of the mountain, the warbler's song, snow on plum blossoms, the plover skimming the Omi Sea—all present a sense of beauty and longing that can be known only in the context of the transient moment caught in the infinite time-frame of the poem. But they are not symbols. The moon is the moon. Saigyō's "sweet loneliness" is available to anyone who has embraced a reclusive life. If we view the world through a lateral rather than a lineal lens of time, Saigyō speaks a living tongue, his world no more a dream than myself, naked this morning, fresh from the bath, mist falling on the moss garden outside a window on the eastern shore of the north Pacific Rim. All "three thousand worlds" grew sud-

denly bright as the dawn sun broke, for only
a moment, between the mountains and the
clouds. The poem never ends.

Notes on the Poets

ARIWARA NO MOTOKATA (fl. ca. 880) was the son of Ariwara no Muneyana. He is known largely through his poems in the *Kokinshū*.

ARIWARA NO NARIHIRA (825–880) was the fifth son of Prince Abo, who was the son of Emperor Heizei and Princess Ito. But Narihira and his brothers were made commoners in 826. He was described as handsome and totally self-indulgent, and figures prominently in *Tales of Ise*. He was one of the "six poetic geniuses" *(rokkasen)*.

FUJIWARA ARIIE (1155–1216) was an early Kamakura poet and one of the compilers of the *Shinkokinshū*. Only twenty of his poems have survived.

FUJIWARA NO TADAFUSA (d. ca. 928) held various court offices and was renowned for his flute playing.

FUJIWARA NO TOKIHIRA (d. 909) rose to the level of Minister of the Left.

FUJIWARA NO TOSHIYUKI (d. ca. 905) held various offices between 866 and his death. He was famous for his calligraphy and was one of the first great *waka* poets.

FUJIWARA OKIKAZE (fl. ca. 900) was equally famous for his paintings on screens and for his music. Emperor Uda was his patron.

FUJIWARA SHUNZEI (1114–1204), one of the most important poets of the *Shinkokinshū*, was a close personal friend and teacher of Saigyō and an influential critic credited with promoting the quality of *yugen*, an "aesthetic feeling not explicitly expressed," or the dark sense of mystery often found in sumi painting, and for adding the element of *sabi*, essential loneliness, to his waka.

FUN'YA NO YASUHIDE (fl. during 9th century) was one of the "six poetic geniuses" *(rokkasen)*.

FURU NO IMAMICHI (fl. late 9th century) held various government positions over more than forty years.

HENJŌ (816–890) was one of the "six geniuses of poetry" *(rokkasen)*. The grandson of Emperor Kanmu and son of Prince Yasuyo, his lay name was Yoshimune no Munesada, but he left court life to become a Buddhist following the death of Emperor Ninmyo in 850, taking the name Henjō. He became a "high priest," or *sojō*, in 885. He is rumored to have carried on an intense love affair with the poet Ono no Komachi.

IKKYŪ SŌJUN (1394–1481) was one of the great poets and Zen masters in all of Japanese literature. Appointed headmaster at Daitokuji, Kyoto's huge temple complex, he reigned nine days before denouncing the monks for hyprocrisy and inviting them to argue their differences "in the whorehouses and sake parlors" where he could be found. A great musician, he was also one of the greatest calligraphers. At seventy he fell in love with a blind singer forty years his junior and scandalized the Buddhist community by moving her into quarters in his temple. He returned to Daitokuji to supervise its reconstruction following a terrible fire. He and his circle made profound contributions to Japanese culture: his friend Murata Shuko was the foremost theorist of the tea ceremony; his friend Iio Sōgi was the greatest master of linked verse; his friend Komparu Zenchiku brought Zen to the Noh drama; the "Sōgi School" of ink painting was made up entirely of Ikkyū's students; and he revolutionized *shakuhachi* (bamboo flute) music.

IMAGAWA RYŌSHUN (1325–1420) authored a small manual for writers called "Treatise of Two Words" (*Nigonshō*) in 1403, and "Ryōshun's Poetics" in 1410.

IZUMI SHIKIBU (970–1030) was the daughter of a feudal lord. *Shikibu* is a title, not a personal name. She was sent to the Heian court to serve a former empress. Her "Diary" details court life and her correspondence and love life in poetry. Famous for her many lovers, including at least two princes, she left court life forever when she married (for a second time) at the age of thirty-six. Lady Murasaki details her animosity toward Izumi in *Tale of Genji*.

JAKUREN (1139–1202) was a priest and a *Shinkokin-shū* poet, and a nephew of Fujiwara Shunzei.

JUSAMMI CHIKAKO (fl. ca. 1300) was a court lady and a follower of Kyōgoku Tamekane. Her poem in this book is from the fourteenth imperial anthology, *Gyōkuyōshū* (ca. 1313).

KAKINOMOTO NO HITOMARO (fl. 8th century) lived during the reign of Emperor Mommu and is the first major poet of the *Man'yōshū*. Little is known of his life except for evidence drawn from his poems. He is considered the master of the *naga-uta,* or middle-length elegy, and the *chōka,* or long poem. He was the first "deified" poet, and his burial place, "the Uta Mound," is considered a holy place. His major poems reveal his deep sense of history and compassionate social conscience.

KAMO NO CHŌMEI (1153–1216) "abandoned the world" to live in a hut in the western mountains within walking distance of Kyoto. He is the author of the *Hojoki,* an account of life in a "ten-foot-square hut," and the *Mumyōshō,* one of the first poetry manuals. He chronicled the devastating fire in the capital in 1177 and the two-year-long famine beginning in 1181.

KENGEI (fl. ca. 875–900) was a priest from Shirogami in Yamato province.

KI NO AKIMINE lived during the late 9th century. His poem is from the *Kokinshū*.

KI NO TOMONORI (d. ca. 906) was the cousin of the poet Ki no Tsurayuki and one of the compilers of the *Kokinshū,* but died before the work was completed. He held various medium-level bureaucratic positions. He was one of the "thirty-six poetic geniuses" (*sanjurokkasen*).

KI NO TSURAYUKI (died ca. 945) is one of the compilers of the *Kokinshū* and one of its major contributors: in addition to a hundred of its poems, he wrote the *kana* (Japanese-language) Preface, one of the most famous statements on poetry in all of Japanese literature: "Poetry begins in the heart." His *Tosa Diary* was a source of inspiration for Bashō and other later poets.

KIYOHARA FUKAYABU (900–930) was a secretary of the palace storehouse.

KŌHŌ KENNICHI (1241–1316) was the son of Emperor Go Saga. He was a member of the Gozan (Five Mountains) group of Zen poets in Kyoto, contributed to several imperial anthologies, and was the teacher of Musō Soseki.

KYŌGOKU TAMEKANE (1254–1332) lived during the collapse of the military government in Kamakura. He advocated a poetics of political and social engagement as well as of philosophical and religious implication, a poetics in search of intensity. He was schooled in the poetry of Su Tung-p'o and other early Chinese Zen poets, and in the first imperial Japanese anthology, *Man'yōshū*.

MANSEI (fl. ca. 730), also called Kasamaro, was a *Man'yōshū* poet and friend and collaborator of Otomo no Yakamochi. He left high court office to become a Buddhist monk.

MIBU NO TADAMINE (ca. 920) was one of the compilers of the *Kokinshū* and held various low-level government positions. He is generally credited with introducing the idea of *yugen* ("aesthetic feeling not directly expressed") to Japanese poetry.

MIKUNI NO MACHI was a minor imperial concubine of Emperor Ninmyo, who lived during the early tenth century.

MOTOORI NORINAGA (1730–1801) was one of Japan's greatest scholars, and his critical commentary on *Tale of Genji* remains a monument. He also "reconstructed" (or translated) the very early Shinto historical text, *Kojiki*. He studied medicine in Kyoto, and continued to practice even as he became more and more deeply engaged in literary endeavors. He lived in the village of Matsuzaka, near Ise, and advocated a poetics based upon the tenth-century *Kokinshū*, stressing the quality of *mono no aware*, the beauty of temporal moments.

MUSŌ SOSEKI (1275–1351) was, along with Saigyō, Ikkyū, and Ryōkan, one of the great Zen poets in all of Japanese literature. Born to a remote branch of the Genji clan, he was related to the powerful Ashikagas. He campaigned tirelessly to preserve Zen traditions. His first Zen teacher was Chinese, and Musō "failed miserably" at his studies. But under the guidance of Kōhō Kennichi, he achieved enlightenment in

1305. He founded Tenryu Temple west of Kyoto in 1339.

ŌE NO CHISATO (ca. 900) rose to the level of provisional vice-governor of Iyo despite having been previously imprisoned. A Confucian scholar, he published a collection of poems in 894.

PRINCESS ŌKU was born in 661 and is the older half sister of Prince Otsu. She served as vestal virgin at Ise Shrine from the age of 14 to 26. She lived the remainder of her life in Kyoto, and died in 701 at the age of 41.

ONO NO KOMACHI (fl. mid-9th century) was the only female member of the "six poetic geniuses." Little is known of her life, except that she was an aristocrat whose beauty was as legendary as her passion. There are

several Noh dramas based upon legends
of her life. Her poetry is especially prized
for her use ,of the "cutting" or "pivot"
word *(kakekotoba)*.

ŌSHIKŌCHI NO MITSUNE (fl. early 10th century) was
known for writing poems with Tsurayuki,
Tadamine, and other court poets, and for
his excursions to various shrines and fa-
mous sites. One-hundred-ninety-three of
his poems survive in various anthologies.

OTOMO NO YAKAMOCHI (718–785) was a major
Man'yōshū poet credited with being one of
its primary editors. Books 17 through 20
represent a chronological arrangement of
his poems and those of his close friends.
He held various high offices, including
that of Commanding General of the East-
ern Armies.

RYŌKAN (1758–1831) was a monk in the Soto branch of Zen. Though a true Zen master, he never headed a temple, living instead by his begging bowl and by patronage, walking throughout the northeastern "snow country" of Niigata province. A renowned calligrapher, he is also said to have bounced a children's silk ball higher than anyone. He took as a Zen name Daigu, or Big Fool. Most of his poetry and calligraphy appears to have been spontaneous, and given away. In addition to his poems in Chinese, his haiku and tanka, he is famous for a four-word, two-line poem inscribed on a kite during one of his journeys: "Above heaven/big winds." In his old age, he fell in love with a young nun with whom he exchanged love poems. He

ended his days as a groundskeeper at a
Shinto Shrine.

SAIGYŌ (1118–1190) was born to a minor branch
of the Fujiwara clan, a family famous for
producing soldiers, but took Buddhist
vows at the age of twenty-three. During
his lifetime, the Heian court collapsed and
the rule of the shoguns began. He is one
of the originators of what might be called
Zen nature poetry. His influence on poets
such as Ikkyū, Bashō, and Ryōkan was pro-
found.

SENGAI GIBBON (1750–1837) was a Zen master
renowned for his calligraphy and for his
predominantly humorous caricatures, most
of which were drawn during the last years
of his life after he retired as Abbott of
Shofukuji, the oldest Zen temple in Japan.

SŌCHŌ (1448–1532) was a student of and companion to Sōgi for more than forty years, a devotee of Ikkyū, and the author of travel diaries that influenced Bashō and others. If his renga is less polished than that of Sōgi, his mind is more original. Like Ikkyū, he thumbed his nose at convention, fathering two children while belonging to a celibate Shingon sect.

SŌGI (1421–1502) was a *renga* (linked verse) master whose travel journals were a source of inspiration and a model for Bashō (especially Bashō's *Oku no hosomichi,* or *Narrow Road to the Interior*). His name is linked forever with Kyushu Island (which he called by its old name, Tsukushi) and the northern Shirakawa Barrier.

SOSEI (d. ca. 909), whose lay name was Yoshimine

no Hironobu, was the son of Henjō. In addition to being a priest, he was revered for his poems combined with images painted on standing screens. Sixty of his poems are included in the *Kokinshū*.

PRINCESS TAJIMA flourished ca. 680–700.

TAKAMURA NO ASON (fl. late 10th century) is a minor *Kokinshū* poet.

TAKAYASU NO ŌSHIMA (fl. late 7th century) is also known only through his few *Man'yōshū* poems.

TSUKAN (782–865) was an early Chinese Zen master (Chinese name: Te-shan) famous for his strict manner. He stressed the importance of being "at oneness with work" or *buji* (Chin., *wu-shih*), or completely free of self-awareness. My translation is based upon an unaccredited early Japanese translation of the Chinese original, a four-line "traditional" poem.

YOSANO AKIKO (1878–1942) was a prolific writer of poetry, novels, essays, fairy tales, translations, and an autobiography. She was in the forefront in the women's rights movement. Her most famous book is a collection of mostly erotic tanka published in 1901, *Midaregami* "Tangled Hair").

PRINCESS YOZA (fl. late 7th century) is among the early contributors to the *Man'yōshū*. She was from a lower "fourth rank" of the imperial court, and died during the summer of 706.